THEY CALL ME LODI

NANCY LEE DE LONG

ISBN: 1539854671

ISBN-13: 9781539854678

DEDICATION

Melissa Zudweg Borden – The Devoted Barn
Joel Rockey – One Last Treat
Zach Skow – Marley's Mutts Dog Rescue

Hi! They call me Lodi (pronounced Low-DEE).

Well as of August 17, 2016. Before that I was known as Panda. I guess my black and white coloring resembles a panda bear. Although I've never seen one, so I can't be sure. I haven't been on this earth too long – so I still have a lot to learn. I was born June 2, 2016 sometime between 10 a.m. and noon. I have six siblings, although all my brothers and sisters have since found their fur-ever homes. I lived with my Mama and her human in Lodi (pronounced Low-DIE), California.

We were on the road a lot. I didn't mind it. There was always a lot to see and tons of smells that kept my puppy nose busy. Mama's human always made sure me and Mama ate dinner. My mama liked to ride on her human's scooter, but I preferred to run until I got too tired. I kind of think it was too hard for Mama's human to keep up with me.

Now as luck would have it, while me, my mama and her human were hanging out in a parking lot in Lodi (*the city*), this nice lady and her friend were on the side of the highway because their truck broke down. (*Not nice that their truck broke down, but nice that it happened near me.*) But I believe that things happen for a reason. The Universe can be tricky like that. So there we were, me, Mama and her human in this parking lot taking a rest. Mama and I were running around stretching our legs. Then I saw this nice lady run across the street toward us and I got really excited! She was so pretty and was very friendly. I couldn't stop wiggling around, I was so happy! She didn't realize Mama and I had our human with us and she was very worried at first. But then she saw that we weren't alone and she was relieved.

It was a hot day and she wanted to make sure we all had water and to make sure we were not going to run into the street. She spent a long time talking to Mama's human about me and my Mama. She wanted to know where we lived and when I was born and everything like that. Mama's human told her he was looking for a fur-ever home for me, just like he did for all of my siblings. She was so nice and so pretty and she told Mama's human that she would take me with her! I was excited, but kind of scared and sad that I was going to leave my Mama, but I was so happy to go ride in the big red truck and go on new adventures!

She gave my Mama's human some green paper and made sure he had food and water for Mama. She picked me up and she was so nice and comfortable and I knew I was going to be okay with this nice lady and her friend in the big red truck.

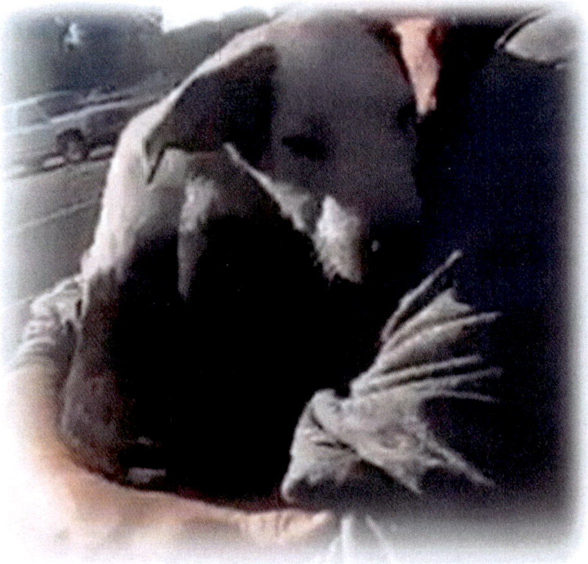

She carried me across the really busy street and put me in the nice cool red truck. Imagine my surprise when I found out there were other fur babies riding in that big truck. There were five other dogs of all shapes and sizes inside that big red doghouse on wheels!

The other dogs' names' were Bandit, Penny, Rue, Samson (he was kind of grumpy) and Seanna. Seanna was the only big dog and she was in a riding cage. My new "mama" put me in the cage with her. I was okay with that because I was still kind of nervous and Seanna was really nervous so we tried to keep each other company. We were both on a new adventure and we didn't know where we were going, but I knew I trusted this nice lady with all of my puppy being.

The nice man finally got the big red truck fixed. Behind the truck he was pulling a big doghouse! It was the biggest doghouse I had ever seen. After we drove, we would stop at night time and everyone would go in the doghouse to eat and sleep. I got to get out of the cage inside there and tried to play with the other dogs. They were all a lot older than I was so they didn't like to play as much. I tried to respect them, but sometimes my puppy-ness would get the better of me.

We were all safe inside that big doghouse and we all had a comfortable bed and food and water and treats too!! When we went to sleep, I got to keep Seanna company, but the other dogs would sometimes sleep with the humans. I was more comfortable with Seanna though.

I really liked the man driving the big red truck. He was really funny. He pretended not to like me, but I knew he was just joking.

The nice lady and the funny man said we had a long way to drive. We were going to some place called The Devoted Barn in Michigan. I don't know what a Michigan is, but I guess I would find out.

Along the way though, we got to make a lot of stops and get out and play. We went to this place that had a big water dish. But the water moved back and forth and it was kind of scary but fun. They called it Lake Tahoe.

We got to run around and play in the water and the sand. It was me, Bandit, Penny and Rue. Samson and Seanna stayed in the big doghouse behind the big red truck. Samson was always so grumpy. He didn't like to play with me.

And they gave me a really pretty pink bandana to wear. I have never worn anything like that before. I thought I looked pretty cute.

Here is the nice man holding as many of us as he could. I kept giving him kisses. He pretended not to like them, but I know he did, because he kept laughing.

The next day, we stopped out in the middle of nowhere. There were no people or cars or doghouses around anywhere. It was hot, but they made sure we always had enough water to drink. The funny man would take us out and let us run. I guess that was so we would sleep when we were back in the big red truck.

We also stopped somewhere called Idaho. The nice lady had a friend there and we stopped to visit her at her house. Seanna got to come out with me in Idaho, but she had to stay attached to one of the humans. She was still kind of scared of everything.

I always made sure to give the funny man a bunch of kisses. He always liked to grab me and play.

After that stop in Idaho, we had a lot of driving to do. We would stop when we had to go outside or to run, but we mainly stayed in the big red truck and slept in the big doghouse at night.

A few days later we made it to the place they called Michigan and The Devoted Barn. The nice lady said this was home. They let me out to explore and there were some funny looking dogs there! They made a funny noise that sounded like "Baaaaa."

One of them was really little and drank out of a baby bottle. I kept trying to see what was in the bottle and see if I could drink out of it too, but they wouldn't let me.

We didn't have to stay in the big doghouse any more. Seanna got to stay in a really big doghouse, but it didn't move, like the other doghouse did. I still stayed in that doghouse a lot of the time. Sometimes the other dogs came in there too, but sometimes they were somewhere else.

They let Seanna come out and explore with me too. That was nice for me. She was my friend. We had kept each other company while we were on our adventures. We both had been kind of scared, and it was nice to be able to curl up and sleep next to her. I sometimes still missed my Mama so it was nice to have her around.

There were a lot of really nice humans at The Devoted Barn. Everybody loved me and I liked to make them smile and laugh. I could always find someone to play with. A lot of the other dogs there didn't like me much though. They kept saying I had too much energy. I don't know what that is, but it must not have been too bad. I think I still have it and it doesn't hurt, so that's a good thing.

A few weeks after we got to the barn, they kept telling me I was getting something called "adopted." I didn't know what that meant. Maybe it was a new friend? A new toy? The nice pretty lady had a lot of nice friends and one of them decided I should go live with her. I still come back and visit my friends at The Devoted Barn though when I can. And I still love to kiss the funny man.

Here I am with my new fur-ever mom. She makes me very happy.

It's been a crazy adventure for me and I'm not even six months old yet. I was so lucky to have so many loving and caring humans around me. From my own mama's human who did his best to take care of me and then the nice pretty lady and the funny man with the big red truck and the big doghouse. I won the puppy lottery that day in Lodi, California. Miracles do happen and the Universe will make them happen for us fur babies and the humans who refuse to give up on us.

"Dogs do speak, but only to those who know how to listen."

~ Orhan Pamuk

About The Devoted Barn:
The Devoted Barn is an animal rescue and rehabilitation facility in Newport, Michigan. Animals from all kinds from cruelty, neglect, and large scale hoarding cases have a chance to find comfort and solace and the opportunity of a new life after spending time at the barn. Animals that are unowned and/or have a need for urgent medical attention get the treatment and love they need and deserve. In addition to these cases, there is also have a large feral dog program in place. These animals come to The Devoted Barn to heal both physically and emotionally. They learn to trust and love again, and some experience that for the first time in their lives. . In addition to helping the animals, their mission is to teach compassion and empathy to others through working with the animals. The Devoted Barn is a place where broken animals and broken people mingle and truly help each other. It is a true safe haven.

About the author:
Nancy Lee De Long is a freelance writer, martial artist and avid animal lover. She began following The Devoted Barn a year ago via Marley's Mutts Dog Rescue, and became a fast friend. She currently lives in Southern California with Applesauce, her golden retriever; Dora, her ninja-hunting calico cat and plays Mother Goose to help care for a gaggle of Chinese Geese at a local park.

43669033R00019

Made in the USA
San Bernardino, CA
22 December 2016